MORE EFFECTIVE CHOIR MINISTRY

A Manual for Church Musicians

Dean C. Schield

SAGAMORE BOOKS
Grand Rapids, Michigan 49508

Copyright ©1986 by Dean C. Schield
All rights reserved.
No part of this booklet may be reproduced without the written permission of the publisher.

Published by Sagamore Books, Inc.
P.O. Box 195, Grand Rapids, MI 49588-0195

Library of Congress Cataloging-in-Publication Data

Schield, Dean C., 1936-
   More effective choir ministry.

   1. Choral singing--Instruction and study.
I. Title.
MT875.S285   1986   783.8   86-42932
ISBN 0-937021-02-4

Printed in the United States of America
87 88 89 90 / 10 9 8 7 6 5

PREFACE

More Effective Choir Ministry began as a simple and practical manual which was given to each person involved in the music/worship ministry of our church, including each choir member, instrumentalist, usher, and sound engineer. This book has grown out of the 27 years in which I have been involved in leading and planning worship, and serving as minister of music.

I found that such a manual, setting forth the philosophy of what we are about in the music/worship ministry, could address problems before they arose. It helped to set forth the purpose from which we jointly and cooperatively ministered through music and worship.

I am convinced that worship is best understood when we take deliberate time to study its purpose, its elements, and its concepts. In most things, we tend to learn by experience. But with worship, we only experience what we understand. We learn much more about worship outside the actual worship experience. We practice and bring to each worship encounter what we have previously learned. The more knowledge we have about worship, the more we will be able to bring greater understanding to the worship celebration.

Worship is a creative art form, and the elements of worship come from a deliberate planning and understanding of these elements.

I envision this book primarily as a practical tool for the implementation of understanding worship. Its particular value will come as it assists you in conceptualizing your own ministry through worship and music.

Worship is CELEBRATION.

Dean C. Schield
Clayton, Ohio

CONTENTS

    Preface 5
1. Worship Is— 7
2. The Role of the Choir in Worship: A Worship Leader ... 13
3. Disciplines of the Choir 16
4. Practical Postures as the Choir Enters 18
5. Achieving a Quality Music Program 20
6. Solos, Duets, Trios, Quartets, and Ensembles 27
    Sample Rehearsal Planning Sheets 30

1.
Worship Is—

I BELIEVE we should begin our study of the music ministry by considering the purpose of a congregation's worship service. Why do we come together for worship? What should happen in the worship service? What is worship?

Worship Is—Celebration

We celebrate what God *HAS* done through Jesus Christ—when Jesus rose from the grave, victorious over sin and over death. We celebrate what God *IS* doing—now, in the present. Jesus is alive today, and He is living in the heart of every believer. We celebrate what God *SHALL* do—in the future. We can praise and thank Him in advance for what He is going to do, for every promise in His word that He will fulfill. Our primary day of corporate worship is Sunday, because that is the day Jesus Christ rose from the grave. Foremost in our celebration is the fact that Jesus is ALIVE!

Our worship and celebration has its background in the Old Testament, and the significance of it is profound even in our present age. In 2 Chronicles 5:13-14 we read about the celebration of worship that transpired on the day Solomon's Temple was dedicated:

> Indeed it came to pass, when the trumpeters and singers were as one, to make one sound to be heard in praising and thanking the Lord, and when they lifted up their voice with the trumpets and cymbals and instruments of music, and praised the Lord, saying: "For He is good, For His mercy endures forever," that the house, the house of the Lord, was filled with a cloud, so that the priests could not continue ministering because of the cloud; for the glory of the Lord filled the house of God (NKJV).

It seems to me that God was so pleased, so delighted, so honored, that He sent down His glory in the form of a visible cloud.

We can be sure that He is still so pleased, so delighted, so honored with our celebration of worship today that He continues to send down His glory, even if not in the form of a visible cloud. For Jesus said, "Where two or three are gathered together in My name, there am I in the midst of them." The size of the group is not important. What is important is that God eagerly looks for those who will worship Him in spirit and in truth. John 4:23-24 states:

> But the hour is coming, and now is, when the true worshipers will worship the Father in spirit and truth; for the Father is seeking such to worship Him. God is Spirit, and those who worship Him must worship in spirit and truth (NKJV).

God's glory may not be seen as a visible cloud in this day; it is, however, sensed and felt through our spiritual being. God is not indifferent to our worship.

We need to worship. Our humanness depends on it. Not to worship God is to deny our essential humanity. It is of the very essence of authentic humanness to worship God. Made to worship we become something less than human when we refuse to worship.

Because worship *is* celebration, our worship experiences must be positive and uplifting. There is no room for any negative thought. One could refer to a worship celebration as an awe-inspiring, joyous, highly serious, deeply earnest, reverent experience.

A celebrative worship service evidences the sort of attitude that a child has as he approaches the celebration of his birthday. When a child asks with a gleam in his eyes, "Guess what today is?", one does not have to ponder the question at any length. It is his birthday! He feels important. He is someone. And today he is going to celebrate with a birthday party. It is with that kind of attitude we should approach our worship experience. We are important. We are someone in God's sight. We are joyfully anticipating meeting God in worship—to celebrate.

We celebrate the fact that Christ has already won the victory. If we really believe what we preach, if we really believe that God is able in this day to deliver every soul, then we must celebrate that victory. Our worship must be positive; it must set forth the example to future generations that God is able to meet human needs. He is meeting our needs, and He is able to meet the needs of those who will serve Him in future generations.

Worship Is—The Offering of Thanksgiving and Praise

The Psalmist David said in Psalms 100, "Make a joyful noise unto the Lord all ye lands. Serve the Lord with gladness; Come before His presence with singing" (KJV). Psalm 95 states, "Oh come, let us sing unto the Lord: let us make a joyful noise to the rock of our salvation. Let us come before his presence with thanksgiving, and make a joyful noise unto him with psalms . . . O come, let us worship and bow down: let us kneel before the Lord, our maker" (KJV).

Paul tells us in Ephesians 5:19-20: "Speak out to one another in psalms and hymns and spiritual songs, offering praise with voices [and instruments], and making melody with all your heart to the Lord. At all time and for everything giving thanks in the name of our Lord Jesus Christ to God the Father" (Amp.).

From the biblical perspective, no person is exempt from the offering of thanksgiving and praise, regardless of the quality of voice or musical training.

Down through the ages, men have responded to the greatest Being they have sensed in the universe, with music and song. Virgil E. Foster writes:

> Of all our response to God in reverence and love, one of the most enjoyable is that in which the whole being expresses its praise and commitment in music and song— a song that stretches every fiber of a person in giving the best that is in him to the God who gave him life, then gave it to him again, abundantly, in Christ.

Worship Is—Obedient Action

Worship is a verb, not a noun—it is active, not passive. It is an act that every person must make in response to the searching lovingkindness of God; for God has acted first, seeking us in many ways to reconcile us to Himself, long before we were ready to seek Him. As a result of God's acts, we are called to action, individually and corporately.

When Moses stood before the burning bush, he was commanded to take off his shoes because he stood on holy ground. His first act was inspired by the presence of the living God; but then Moses was expected to put on his shoes and lead the children of Israel out of the land of Egypt.

Merely to be awestruck in the presence of God is imperfect and inadequate worship. Along with awe, praise, adoration, and thanksgiving must go confession of sin, listening to God's Word, and finally the consecration and dedication of oneself to the tasks to which he is called.

Worship Is—Creative Action

Worship is an act that each person must make creatively. Thus, the worship hour is no stronger than the Spirit-led creativeness of the worship leader in his or her planning and preparation, and in the excellence with which the worship activity is actually done. C. Harry Causey, in his book, *Open the Doors*, states:

> Whatever the worship experience is to be, in whatever style it may be manifest, no matter how small or how large the forces may be that the worship leaders have at their disposal, all must be done with excellence—not perfection—or we would always fail.

Our worship experiences need to be creative and of the highest quality. Nothing but our *best* should be offered to God in praise and adoration of Him.

Worship should be orderly. Since all parts of the worship experience serve as vehicles for the communion of God with man and man with God, worship should be done with regard to decency and propriety, in an orderly fashion, as Paul wrote in 1 Corinthians 14:40. God is a God of order. Our worship services should have order, planned creativity, without restrictive form.

Worship itself is a creative action. Our minds and hearts are seeking signs of God—His presence, His goodness, His loving care—so that we will be able to respond. Unless we worship with expectancy, we will have eyes and see not, and ears and hear not. In the words of Elizabeth Barrett Browning in "Aurora Leigh":

> Earth's crammed with heaven,
> And every common bush afire with God;
> And only he who sees takes off his shoes—
> The rest sit round it and pluck blackberries.

Awareness of the burning bush was crucial to the encounter of Moses with God, and the people of Israel depended on his perception. But surely, we would say, a burning bush would be easy to see;

no one could miss that. Yet, week after week, the typical Christian congregation is in the presence of God—repeating holy words, handling holy things—till constant, thoughtless repetition dulls the mind into a rote performance of a high and holy exercise. We "sit and pluck blackberries."

Only as each person allows God to "make all things new" in each worship experience can true worship take place. The most familiar parts of the worship experience should be approached with a fresh and creative mind, and the unfamiliar parts should be welcomed with an open and receptive mind.

Worship Is—Interaction Between God and Man

God acts first, but man also acts in worship, and his actions take several personal and corporate forms. For example, in a service of worship, the singing of a hymn may be an act of giving thanks, of confessing, of praying for guidance, or of consecrating oneself to the will of God. And while that hymn is being corporately sung, each individual must make a personal appropriation of its message to himself if it is to have its fullest meaning and value. Each person must make his own offering of praise and prayer to God, just as each person must face the judgment and will of God. Each individual has a unique and personal act of worship which he alone can offer before God.

Worship recognizes the sovereignty and majesty of God, and the lordship of Jesus Christ; it also recognizes the ministry of the Holy Spirit. In our services of worship, the Holy Spirit ministers to the different needs of the congregation. When one person is hurting, the Holy Spirit can direct a thought from a hymn, a prayer, the Word, or the sermon to that person. At the same time, the identical hymn, the identical prayer, the identical Scripture, the identical sermon can minister to another person whose needs are completely different. This is the uniqueness of the Holy Spirit's work in worship.

The Holy Spirit honors our creative efforts by ministering to each individual need of the congregation during the worship experience. For this reason, one does not have to be overly concerned about choosing a particular song for the bereaved and discouraged, then choosing another song for those who are experiencing euphoria. What better place for a bereaved family to be on a Sunday morning than in the house of God, singing His praises, with the full assurance that God will come to their aid and fulfill His promises, even during the most trying and difficult moments in life? What better place for a joyous person to be on a Sunday morning than in the house of God, singing His praises, thanking Him for all the blessings they have received, knowing that God wants the very best for His people?

Worship Is—Reaction

Worship that is honest, worthy, creative, and based on faith will result not only in action and interaction, but also in faithful reaction. It is stirring to talk with God; but it is equally important that we hear His commands and obey.

True worship calls from us the same response that Isaiah had in the temple, as recorded in Isaiah 6:8. This is probably the classic example of response. Isaiah came into the temple to worship with much the same attitude that most people have as they arrive at worship today. His king had died and there was no leadership in the land. Isaiah was discouraged, he was low in spirit. But he heard the voice of the Lord that day. He felt God's presence. He was reflective. He reflected his convictions, first, by where he was and, second, by the mood he was in. But finally, he was responsive to God, who was victorious. Isaiah's inward feeling became an outward expression. God said, "Who will I send? Who will go for us?" Isaiah said, "Here am I, Lord; send me."

God may show His will to us at moments when we do not necessarily want to know the will of God. An opportunity must be given in all services of worship for each person to respond—respond to all that he has heard, all that he has felt, all that he has understood, and to the challenge that has been extended.

Response can take many forms: thanksgiving, praise, giving of tithes and offerings, obedience to God's commands, determination to serve God in a greater capacity. But the greatest response that can happen during a worship experience is a person's acceptance of the plan of salvation through Jesus Christ.

True worshipers will respond with nothing but the best—in worship, in life, and in service.

2.
The Role of The Choir in Worship: A Worship Leader

THE most important aspect of being an effective choir member is to understand that you, first of all, are a worship leader. The purpose of the choir is to help bring a sense of celebration to the worship of God, to prompt the congregation in singing praise to God, to prompt those in the congregation in their effort to become creative worshipers. To do this most effectively, each choir member should grasp an understanding of the role of the choir as a prompter in the worship experience.

Too often, the choir assumes the role of being a *performer* on the platform, their main purpose being to sing a stirring anthem to the *audience*, all of which is being *prompted* by God. We mistakenly suppose that those on the platform are the performers; that the congregation is the audience, spectators to the great performance being done by the platform people; and that God is up in heaven, prompting the performers.

Soren Kierkegaard taught that there is indeed drama in worship, but the platform is not the stage. The real stage from which the drama comes forth is the heart and life of each person in the assemblage (in the congregation *and* on the platform), who gives praise and worship to God.

God is not the prompter or director of this drama. *God is the audience.*

The choir, the instrumentalists, and the pastors are the *prompters*, prompting each person gathered for worship in giving his best to God, the Creator. The worshiping congregation then becomes the true *performers*.

God alone is worthy to receive our worship and praise. He alone deserves to be the audience. Revelation 4:11 states:

> Thou art worthy, O Lord, to receive glory and honor and power: for Thou hast created all things, and for Thy pleasure they are and were created (KJV).

God certainly knows the importance and value of a choir. In biblical times, the choir was used for the most important events and special occasions. A full choir of angels sang, "Glory to God in the highest!" to the shepherds in Bethlehem the night Christ was born. Choirs were set apart to head the musical worship at the dedication of Solomon's temple. In another instance, a choir was used to lead the people in battle against the enemy.

From the beginning of history, music has been joined with man's religious experience. The choir has been one of the most important vehicles through which to express man's praise in musical form, to magnify the glory of God. Music belongs in worship only when it is an offering to God, who is the *audience*.

Each member of the choir should sense a personal ministry through her or his musical participation and service as a worship leader. The Holy Spirit uses the choir to teach, inspire, and convict. The deepest spiritual needs of persons can be reached through music and the ministry of the choir.

The choir member recognizes that the anthem is a prepared musical offering. It is being offered by a well-rehearsed group on behalf of the whole congregation. Each person in the congregation should feel that the anthem is his personal musical offering to God; he should sense that the choir is singing his thoughts and feelings, just as he would like to express them to God, had he the musical ability to do so. Our musical gifts are from God. Our talents are from God. And we use these gifts and talents to create an offering of praise.

The musical expression offered by the choir is a combined effort. The choir is a team, with a common purpose and a common goal. They are all working together to become better qualified leaders in the art of worship, as well as true worshipers. They are striving to become growing Christians through the sharing of their musical experience.

As melody, rhythm, and harmony are joined together in great outpourings of praise and supplication, so should our various lives be united by the indwelling of the Holy Spirit to create a corporate wholeness that is worthy of the high calling of Jesus Christ our Lord.

3.
Disciplines of the Choir

THE term *volunteer* has unfortunate connotations, and its use should be discouraged in connection with the choir. In the first place, one does not "volunteer" to attend church, to contribute to the church budget, or do anything else that returns to God a very small portion of all that He has given to us. Serving God is not an option for the Christian. It is a natural result of what God has done in one's life.

When Jesus told the parable of the talents, He was making a statement of this truth. He indicated that God gives us certain abilities that He expects us to use. If we fail to use them, and fail to glorify Him, we have sinned. "It follows, then, that in the musically mature church, the ministry of choir singing is now regarded as a privilege and a trust." (Taken from *Music and Worship in the Church*, by Loveland and Rice.)

To become most effective, each person in the choir accepts the responsibilities that came with his commitment to this privilege and trust. This commitment demands certain disciplines of time and energy. Commitment to the music ministry means:

1. *Being present at every rehearsal, and present at every service of worship as a worship leader.* We are a blessed people. God has chosen us, set us apart from the world, given us the free gift of eternal life, offered us His presence and power as daily companions. We, then, are eager to be in our place of ministry; we do not look for excuses to be absent from service.

We should remember that a choir member is much more than just a talented soprano, alto, tenor, or bass. Participation in the music ministry means much more than just balancing a particular vocal section (although that is very important for excellent musical expressions). Our motivation to sing in the choir comes from the call of God to be stewards of our God-given talents. We do not attend rehearsals and worship services out of obedience to "choir rules and regulations"; we come in response to a divine call, an inward knowledge that God expects our musical participation.

2. *Being committed to learn, understand, and experience unfamiliar styles and forms of music.* In ministering to the total body of the church, the styles and forms of the choir have to be varied.

3. *Being committed to learn the music as well as possible.* This involves being committed to practice individually on a difficult section; to improve personal skills through disciplined practice; and to take advantage of every opportunity to improve musical skills.

4. *Being committed to take care of the music materials and equipment.* Choir members are expected to treat music folders with care; to cooperate in keeping the rehearsal room neat; to return the music at the requested time; to carefully hang their choir robes; and to insure that their choir robes and folders are in proper place after use.

5. *Being committed to participate in each rehearsal with concentration and attentiveness.* It is only natural for dedicated choir members to be well mannered in the choir rehearsal; to avoid all unnecessary talking; to have a positive attitude; to avoid sarcastic comments, temperamental outbursts, and similar displays of bad manners and unchristian conduct; and to be flexible.

6. *Being committed to watch the director at all times.* This means that one is committed to memorize the music when necessary, to free oneself from constantly having to watch the music. It means that each choir member is ready to cooperate pleasantly in the logistics of rehearsal; to make every effort to follow the director's instructions as to dynamics, pronunciation, rhythm, and so on; to realize that each section of the choir has a right to rehearse; and to make maximum use of every minute of the rehearsal.

7. *Being committed to share in a common cause through the music ministry.* It involves being eager to get acquainted with other choir members; to become caring persons within the choir; to help new choir members feel welcomed, wanted, and needed; to pray for the concerns of the total church family; to care and pray for the ministries of the total church; to be growing Christians; and to take advantage of every opportunity to learn and grow in the Christian faith.

8. *Being committed to allowing the musical experience to be joyful, uplifting, meaningful—and at times, just plain FUN!*

4.
Practical Postures As the Choir Enters

AS WE have seen, the role of the choir is that of a worship leader. Each choir member realizes that maximum efficiency in leading worship is achieved only through certain disciplines. One of those disciplines is the choir's posture as it enters the sanctuary.

Webster defines posture as "the position or bearing of the body, whether characteristic or assumed for a special purpose . . . a conscious mental pose: attitude." The following is a specific, simple, yet necessary list of ideas and suggestions to help the choir attain the necessary posture at the beginning of worship.

1. As you drive to church, pray for the worship hour, for the congregation that will be assembled, and for the needs that will be represented.

2. Put on your choir robe in sufficient time to insure that you can attend a short rehearsal before the service of worship begins.

3. Remove excessive jewelry, scarves, collars, and other items that would distract from the choir's uniform appearance.

4. Make sure you have all of the printed music needed for the service, and an order of worship (when available). Make sure that you are personally ready.

5. Check your choir robe just before entering the sanctuary to assure everything is in order. (Straighten the stole, for example.)

6. Enter the sanctuary and the choir loft with a joyful, positive, reverent attitude. Anticipate God's presence. Look pleasant.

7. Walk erectly with the attitude that you know exactly what you are doing; thus, you assure the congregation that everything is under control.

8. Be orderly as you enter the sanctuary. All of the choir folders should be held in uniform position, for example.

9. Once in your place in the choir loft, stand erect and steady. There should be no moving around to put music down, pick up hymnals, put Bibles down, and so on. Wait until everyone is seated and the attention is off of the choir before getting personally "organized."

10. Smile as you wait for the direction to be seated.

11. Watch the director for all instructions to sit, stand, open folders, and so on. Follow those instructions together.

12. While seated in the choir loft, avoid wiggling, excessive moving around, bending over to pick up books, and so on. Try to pick up hymnals and books as gracefully as possible.

13. Avoid nervous habits (nail biting, leaning forward in your chair, folding arms, slouching, playing with your hair, resting elbows on your knees, and so on).

14. Be attentive during the entire service. Be conscious of the progression of the service and be prepared for each part of the activities. Remember that you are a worshiper as well as a worship leader. Be ready for any changes that might be made during the service.

15. Respond in a quiet, controlled manner to any disturbances which might occur during the worship hour. Don't make a bad incident worse by overreacting.

16. Do not engage in unnecessary talking during the service, especially during the offertory. Talk to God.

17. Enjoy the experience of worship.

18. Remember that you and other members of the choir are human. In case of a mistake, smile. Act as if everything is just fine, and keep going.

This attempt to be careful of our posture is for one simple reason—to insure that our music brings glory to God. Excellent music results from well-applied choir disciplines. But the worthiness of our music will be judged in terms of how well it ministers to people and how well it communicates the gospel of Christ.

5.
Achieving a Quality Music Program

GOETHE wrote, "The quality of the experience resides in the dream; the higher the quality, the greater the obstacles." Certainly this is true of the church's music ministry. The higher the level of quality that we seek to attain, the greater will be the obstacles to attaining it. But, the end in view— glorifying our Lord—deserves our finest efforts.

All of us remember running relay races in our childhood. As we began, someone would bark out the orders: "Ready! Get set! Go!" These phrases can also be a key to achieving a quality music program in the local church.

Ready—The Dream: Planning and Preparation

No quality music program can be achieved without spending time in setting goals. These goals should include the objectives that you would like to see achieved by the choir, by other musical groups, by soloists, and by the total congregation.

We set three types of goals: (1) those that can be reached easily; (2) some that will stretch us, but are achievable; and (3) others that we might not be able to reach. The goals are set and communicated so that everyone concerned will know the direction of the church's total music ministry. This will keep all of the church's musicians centered on achieving the same goals.

The goals may include the presentation of certain musicals; the formation of a sanctuary choir; the scheduling of special concerts; concert tours; recording sessions; music education experiences; formation of an instrumental ensemble; or improving the quality of congregational singing.

After your musical goals have been set, review the resources and personnel you will need in achieving the goals. Know the practical potential of the choir, of the accompanists, of the facilities with which you have to work. Evaluate what you have at hand. Know where to go to get help, if desired.

Then start preparing to reach the goals. Select the printed music you need to achieve the goals. Remember, the music you select should fit your program, meet your needs, strengthen your worship concepts, and be an educational tool. In your music selection, don't try to use everything. Some musical styles and forms will not fit the size of your choir or their musical ability. Find selections that will work for you—music that is in the range of your singers, music that your accompanists and/or instrumentalists will be able to handle after practicing and learning it. Select some music that can be sung at the first reading; select other pieces that will require everyone to work hard. Keep in mind that the choir needs to experience successes in the short-term goals, as you keep working toward the long-term goals that present much more challenge.

Select music that will meet the congregation's needs. Yes, even if that means selecting some hymns which may not be what they want. Help the congregation learn to be comfortable with a variety of styles and forms.

In setting goals for a quality music program, keep in mind that everything is done with a purpose. We must hold firmly to our purpose and message, while varying our methods. We are more concerned about present needs and opportunities than about preserving traditions of the past. We develop a wide base of solid musical leadership, rather than a few "superstars" on whom the whole structure of our ministry rises or falls.

Get Set—Overcoming the Obstacles: The Doing

After setting the goals . . . after selecting, ordering, and having the music in hand . . . after rallying the troops . . . the next step is the doing, the execution of the plan. At this point, there is no substitute for hard work. We must be ready to pay the price for an effective music ministry, for nothing comes easy.

Plan the rehearsal schedule and start working, measure by measure. Be particular with the details. Leave no stone unturned. Drill the music. Rehearse the music. Stretch yourselves by singing the music correctly. That is how to grasp an understanding of what the music is saying.

Learn the intervals. Sing the dynamics. Sing the entire selection through without stopping; and sing the selection through part by part. Do whatever you have to do to achieve your musical goals.

When we are in pursuit of excellence in the music ministry, we will stop at nothing. We hire babysitters; we make costumes; we build sets; we collect props; we talk with audio control people; we schedule and work with lighting experts; we make messes in the church; and we clean up the messes.

We execute the plan with a positive, honest attitude. We are willing to try one way; and if it doesn't work, we discard it and try another way. We teach our musicians to be flexible. We laugh at our mistakes. We hold no resentments.

In achieving a quality music program, the fun and challenge are in overcoming the obstacles. It all comes down to a simple procedure—*doing* the plan. And in all this doing, we learn to love and care for one another.

Go: Results of the Doing

Every quality church music program seems to spawn new ministry opportunities and new responsibilities. These opportunities will mean new people, new places, new programs, and new challenges

New people will be added to your music program. A quality program attracts quality people, and they will bring a variety of skills and talents.

A progressive choir program is contagious. People will hear about it and inquire about it. Whenever inspirational music is needed for group meetings, community events, or patriotic programs, the choir (because of their disciplined "doing" and resulting growth) are ready to minister.

There will be new responsibilities of educating youth and children, to prepare them for service in the local church through the ministry of music. A result of this growth? The development of a solid base of operation, for the perpetuation of the music ministry within the life of the church, from generation to generation.

Long-range goals—in terms of 15 to 25 years—must be considered. Give careful deliberation to ways that you can inspire young people and use their talent within the music ministry of your church.

A progressive music program creates excitement within the church. It enlarges the people's vision for the church; it reinforces

There is at least one person in the congregation who "needs" to hear the music we are singing.

the musician's belief that the church offers the most exciting, inspirational, and challenging opportunities in which Christians can utilize their abilities.

As the choir sings and ministers together, they will begin to know one another and care for one another. With this caring attitude will come new responsibilities of sharing the greater concerns for spiritual maturity in the body.

One way to keep aware of the pulse of this caring attitude is to form a "Touch Team" within the choir. This is simply a few selected, mature members of the choir who will take the responsibility of assuring that each need, concern, or problem of church musicians is recognized. Each person on the Touch Team is assigned a small group of people within the choir, and is responsible for seeing that the lines of communication between the choir members and the director are open at all times. Poor choir attendance and communication problems can easily be solved (or at least recognized) by a simple telephone call from a Touch Team person. The choir is aware that the Touch Team is not there to pry into the affairs of others, but simply to let the choir members know this is a caring group of people who are concerned. The Touch Team acts as the liaison between a moving, exciting choir, and an individual's pressing need.

The Touch Team also helps to assimilate new choir members into the life and operation of the choir. It helps make sure that the "old timers" are not forgotten or taken for granted.

Growth results from the choir's continuous understanding of its reason for existence, which is much more than just singing. The choir operates with a definite purpose, individually and corporately. This community of musicians follows their Lord. They obey God's Word; they worship and glorify God in their celebrations of love, joy, and loyalty. They help people find eternal life. They help people face the most important issues of life. They provide Christians an opportunity to serve.

Growth results from a quality program, which is directly related to the musician's belief in the importance of the local church. Their belief is continuously strengthened with the idea that the local church is one of the most profound and most significant of all places in which to use their musical talents and gifts.

Where else but in the local church do musicians have the opportunity to minister week after week to the lives of hungry, needy people—to the people they know best?

The ultimate mission of our music ministry is not to be on the bus, down the road 40 miles. Our mission is right at home, Sunday after Sunday, in the local church—in services of worship where the best of everyone is required. The musicians involved in a quality music program communicate this conviction to outsiders, and this belief brings new people into the church.

Choir Rehearsals

Since good choir rehearsals are crucial to implementing a more effective church music program, let us pause to consider some specific ways to improve the rehearsal time.

Some of us are blessed with good facilities. Making the choir rehearsal a pleasant experience certainly has a lot to do with physical arrangements. Good lighting, comfortable heating or cooling, seating arrangements in which everyone can see and hear well—these are all important elements to a successful choir rehearsal.

It is imperative that each choir member has a copy of music. It is much too difficult for two or more people to read from a shared copy of music. Make sure enough copies of music are purchased for each member of the choir, plus a few extra copies.

Good rehearsals will only happen from good preparation. The choir director must always know the music well. She or he will already know or can anticipate where the problems will lie, and will have worked out a scheme by which the problems can be solved, before the rehearsal begins.

The director will have shared the music with the accompanists before the rehearsal, to insure that the rehearsal time is not for the accompanists, but for the choir.

The director will plan the order in which the music is to be rehearsed, giving consideration to the voice demand, the emotional pitch and movement of each tune. (Avoid rehearsing back-to-back tunes that call for intense vocal exercise.)

The rehearsal should be planned to give special attention to training. Give opportunity for every musical problem to be worked out.

Begin with a vocal warm-up exercise, followed by a more familiar tune that the choir can sing rather readily, for a sense of security and accomplishment early in the rehearsal. (The choir should always have five to seven tunes rehearsed, in order to keep current.)

It is helpful to use a rehearsal planning sheet, itemizing the rehearsal schedule, the goals to reach during the rehearsal, and the problem spots to be worked through. Alexandria House has prepared a practical form for rehearsal planning, which is very helpful. A copy of this sheet is printed at the back of this booklet for your consideration.

The director should select each piece for the rehearsal with an eye toward the tempo/rhythm, interpretation/dynamics, problem spots, and other features that will have to be considered.

During the rehearsal, let no problem slip by. Correct every error immediately. If the blend, diction, interval, note, pronunciation, or dynamic level is wrong, correct it immediately. Don't let the choir learn a selection improperly. The undoing will take more time later than stopping now to correct problems.

Include in every rehearsal a time of prayer, devotion, and inspirational thoughts. Plan the rehearsal so that it is spiritually uplifting and inspirational.

Spend time together in discussing the concept of each tune. What is it trying to say? What is the best way to say it?

The choir director should encourage moments of humor, moments of comic relief when the choir can laugh at themselves or at the director. The choir director should never be afraid to admit to a mistake, but he should have confidence in his ability to direct, lead, and teach the music well. The director should be in charge of the rehearsal at all times.

Other tips for the director: Stress the importance of memorization. Encourage intense concentration during each rehearsal. Choose music that motivates. Keep the posture of the choir "up". Have them stand occasionally and show them how to sit "tall in the saddle."

Keep the choir singing as much as possible; if you need to rehearse the soprano part, for example, have all the parts sing the soprano line. Help the choir members to become better sight readers. In every way, encourage personal discipline during the rehearsal.

The rehearsal is a good time to convey the expressions of appreciation from congregation members and/or pastors. Bring to the choir's attention newsworthy information of choir members: new babies, job promotions, honors received, engagements, and so on.

Make the rehearsal a time of fun and enjoyment. This is no time for negative comments. Keep everyone in a positive attitude by encouraging and supporting them; encourage singers when they do well, and do not be overly critical when they fall short.

A well-disciplined rehearsal leads to a well-disciplined choir. But let it also be a relaxing, enjoyable time. Do not squelch individual spontaneity.

Always teach the worship concepts during the rehearsal. Use correct worship terminology. Encourage the choir's participation as worship leaders, not just singers. And keep bringing to mind the ministry purpose of the choir.

6.
Solos, Duets, Trios, Quartets, and Ensembles

THE choir is the hub of the music ministry. Therefore, all soloists and ensemble members are loyal, faithful choir persons. Their ministry of music as a soloist or ensemble member is like that of the choir—to *prompt* the congregation in worship celebration.

Soloists and ensemble members are parts of the team, a part of the church's total music ministry. These people have ability, talents, and special gifts that they are expected to share. There is no room for prima donnas or superstars in the church's music ministry. Each singer's value depends upon his or her ability to communicate the gospel through his or her music.

Let me emphasize again that church music is a ministry-centered program. The quality of our ministry varies directly with our ability to minister to needs of the congregation in worship.

Certainly, good sounding, well-trained voices are needed. Certainly, solos and ensemble music can have a vital ministry in worship, and we should always use the best we have in our services of worship. However, these are not the only qualities we seek. The union of voice and spirit makes an all-important difference in a Christian singer's effectiveness.

A good soloist or ensemble member understands that his spirit—blended with the spirit of the song, a recognition of the inspiration of the song, and the reverent way the song is presented—has as much to do with his effectiveness as a well-trained voice singing a well-prepared selection.

As worship leaders, we are always striving to present the *best* that we can do and be. Never do we compromise our musical standards and sacrifice the quality of the worship experience. We use soloists and ensemble members who have been given a natural gift, who have refined it, and are continuing to refine their gift into as excellent quality as they can obtain.

Not everyone should sing solos. Singing a solo is not necessarily a higher calling than other areas in the ministry of music; and everyone who has a good voice is not necessarily a "soloist." It is a simple fact that some people can communicate through a solo better than others.

But with those considerations aside, let us remember that the testimony of each musician's life is as important as the song that is sung. Soloists and ensemble members love their church. Their ultimate goal is to be able to communicate the Word of God in song to the local congregation. Their desire is to build up the local church. They are humble in their service; they are sensitive to how the song can communicate; they understand what needs it will reach and touch. They are aware of their ability to communicate. They know when they do communicate effectively and when they don't. Soloists and ensemble members are growing Christians—loving, caring people with a strong witness.

Let's discuss a few practical things about the work of soloists and ensemble members:

Every song should be *memorized*. How else can a song be communicated, unless the singer has a good knowledge of the song and can use eye contact with the congregation?

The song should speak of your own experience. Then you will spiritually be able to understand the song and communicate its message to the congregation.

Do not choose a song simply because it is someone's favorite, or happens to be in the "top twenty" of current religious hit tunes. Make sure that your song fits into the particular worship service for which you have been asked to sing. Share not only its title, but its content and mood with those responsible for planning the worship service.

Do all that you can to prepare musically for the song. Rehearse with your accompanists and involve any other musicians that will accompany you. (Be sure that the schedule of your rehearsals will not conflict with the other regular music ministry schedules.)

Remember that the message of your song is more important than the voice. Sing with joy. See yourself as another voice of the congregation, bringing praise to God. God must receive the glory; so select the right song—your song. Remember that *God is the audience*.

Make sure you are well groomed and outwardly poised. Respect the people to whom you are singing by making your outward appearance as attractive as possible.

It is certainly not only by our own musical talents that people are touched—but by the power of God flowing through us and our abilities. A soloist or ensemble member then strives for excellence in the music, but realizes that music is not the end in itself; it is only the means for something far greater—for leading people to God and experiencing the reality of His presence.

God is the Audience. The musicians are the Prompters. Those who truly worship are the real Performers.

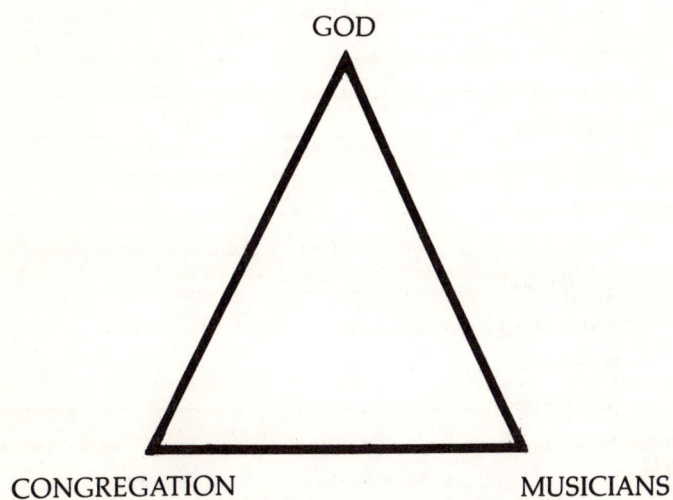

THE ALEXANDRIA HOUSE
REHEARSAL PLANNING SHEET

Date _____

Warm-Up _____
_____
_____

Welcome / Recognitions _____
_____
_____

Selection #1 _____

    Time _____ Performance Date _____ Soloist _____

    Tempo / Rhythm _____

    Interpretation / Dynamics _____

    Problem Spots _____

    Other Comments _____

Selection #2 _____

    Time _____ Performance Date _____ Soloist _____

    Tempo / Rhythm _____

    Interpretation / Dynamics _____

    Problem Spots _____

    Other Comments _____

Selection #3 _____

    Time _____ Performance Date _____ Soloist _____

    Tempo / Rhythm _____

    Interpretation / Dynamics _____

    Problem Spots _____

    Other Comments _____

Used by permission.

P.O. Box 300
Alexandria, Indiana 46001

Alexandria House

Selection #4 _____

    Time _____ Performance Date _____ Soloist _____

    Tempo / Rhythm _____

    Interpretation / Dynamics _____

    Problem Spots _____

    Other Comments _____

Selection #5 _____

    Time _____ Performance Date _____ Soloist _____

    Tempo / Rhythm _____

    Interpretation / Dynamics _____

    Problem Spots _____

    Other Comments _____

Selection #6 _____

    Time _____ Performance Date _____ Soloist _____

    Tempo / Rhythm _____

    Interpretation / Dynamics _____

    Problem Spots _____

    Other Comments _____

Visitors / New Members _____

_____

_____

Announcements _____

_____

_____

Inspirational Thoughts _____

_____

_____

Special Prayer Requests _____

_____

_____